A WALK THROUGH A RAIN FOREST

A WALK THROUGH A RAIN FOREST

LIFE IN THE ITURI FOREST OF ZAIRE

DAVID JENIKE

MARK JENIKE

A CINCINNATI ZOO BOOK

FRANKLIN WATTS

NEW YORK   CHICAGO   LONDON   TORONTO   SYDNEY

DEDICATED TO OUR PARENTS, MARY ANN AND SAM JENIKE

The authors wish to acknowledge the contributions of other researchers to this book. In particular, we thank Bob Bailey, David Wilkie, Sean Thomas, and Nadine Peacock, from whose research we drew heavily.

Photographs copyright © Anthro-Photo/Mark Jenike: p. 24;
S. David Jenike: pp. 28, 29, 30, 35, 37, 39, 40, 41, 43, 53, 54
bottom, 64 top; Wisconsin Regional Primate Research Center,
University of Wisconsin/ Frans DeWaal: p. 33; M. Busching:
p. 34; David S. Wilkie and Gilda Morelli: pp. 36, 48;
Cincinnati Zoo/Ron Austing: p. 54 top; all other photographs
copyright © Mark Jenike.

Library of Congress Cataloging-in-Publication Data

Jenike, David.
A walk through a rain forest : life in the Ituri Forest of Zaire /
David Jenike, Mark Jenike.
p.   cm.—(A Cincinnati Zoo book)
Includes bibliographical references (p.   ) and index.
ISBN 0-531-11168-7 (lib. bdg.)—ISBN 0-531-15721-0 (pbk.)
1. Rain forest ecology—Zaire—Ituri Forest—Juvenile literature.
2. Ituri Forest (Zaire)—Juvenile literature. [1. Rain forest
ecology. 2. Ecology. 3. Ituri Forest (Zaire)]   I. Jenike, Mark.
II. Title.   III. Series.
QH195.C6J46   1994
574.5'2642'096751—dc20   94-29389 CIP AC

Text copyright © 1994 by the Zoological Society of Cincinnati, Inc.

ITURI FOREST

AFRICA

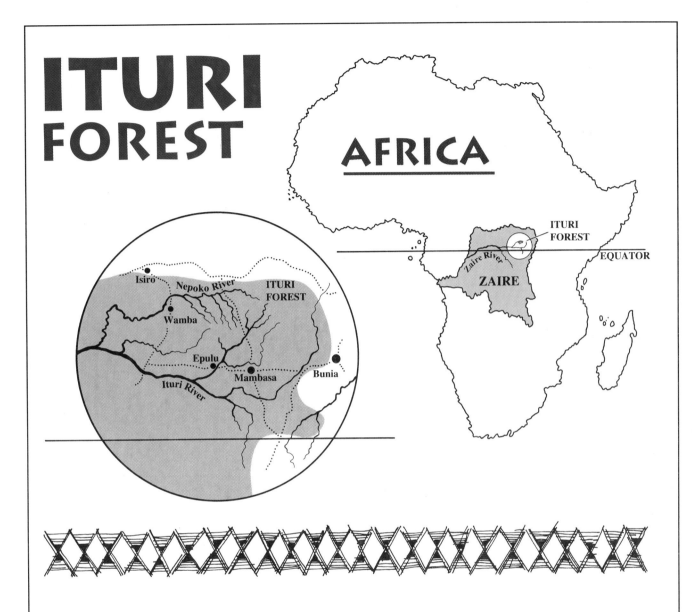

The Ituri Forest lies along the northeast rim of the great depression in the center of Africa that makes up the Zaire River basin, and it is on the edge of the belt of African rain forest that extends from Ivory Coast to the great rift in east-central Africa.

Tropical rain forests lie between the Tropic of Cancer and the Tropic of Capricorn (thus the name tropical) and receive over 60 inches (1.5 m) of rain each year. Because they are close to the equator, they get at least 12 hours of sunlight every day. Sunlight, warm temperatures, and abundant water create an environment that supports an amazing diversity of plant life. The plant life, in turn, supports a wide array of animal species. Over 50 percent of the earth's plant and animal species live in tropical rain forests.

A WALK IN THE ITURI FOREST

From a low-flying airplane crossing over central Africa, the Ituri Forest looks like a head of broccoli, with a series of rounded green clumps packed closely upon each other. Here and there a clump rises above the others and we can see what it is. Each green mound is the top of one giant tree. Standing together the clumps make up a continuous **canopy**, an umbrella of trees shielding the forest floor. This is what all **tropical rain forests** look like from the sky. The Ituri Forest, named for the Ituri River that runs through it, covers about 24,300 square miles (39,123 sq km) in the nation of Zaire, and ranges in altitude from 2,300 to 3,300 feet (700 to 1,000 m) above sea level.

Within the Ituri Forest lives one of the most diverse communities of life on earth. The most influential members of that community, but not the most ancient, are the human farmers and forest **foragers** who have lived in it for at least the last few thousand years. About 2,000 to 4,000 years ago, the ancestors of the farmers moved into the region

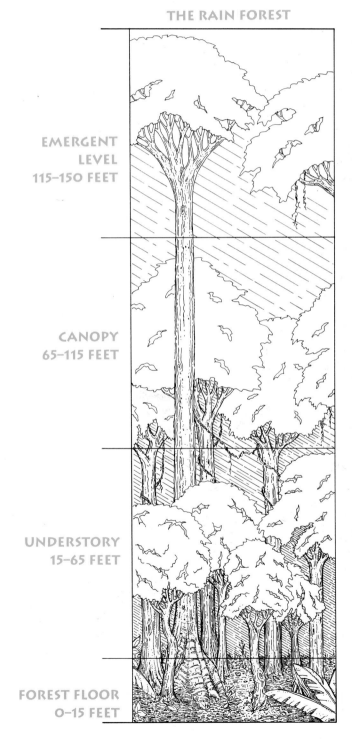

THE RAIN FOREST

EMERGENT LEVEL 115–150 FEET

CANOPY 65–115 FEET

UNDERSTORY 15–65 FEET

FOREST FLOOR 0–15 FEET

that today is the Ituri. The foragers, who probably do not share a recent common ancestry with the farmers, were at this time already living in the Ituri Forest or at its edge. Today the two groups speak different dialects, or local variations, of the same language.

About 50 million **indigenous people** now live in tropical rain forests. The lifeways of many of these peoples still resemble the lifeways of their distant ancestors.

Many Lese farmers live in villages near one of the roads through the Ituri.

The farmers brought with them their skill of working iron into tools. Using a forge made from forest materials, they could melt iron and shape it to form farming tools. Today most of the farmers' tools are made outside the Ituri and are bought from local merchants. However, the farmers do still forge some tools—such as the **apapau**, a blade that is sharpened on one side and is curved into a hook at the end—in the traditional way. With the tools they made, the farmers cleared patches of forest and started gardens. Today their mixed crops include rice, bananas, and **manioc**—a large, potatolike tuber that is an important part of their diet. The farmers' gardening methods were probably unfamiliar to the foragers living in the forest. The foragers collect food directly from the forest, by hunting animals and gathering edible plants.

Today groups of farmers and foragers live near each other in the forest and depend on each other. The farmers live in small, semipermanent villages built in forest clearings. The foragers set up temporary camps in the forest. They build beehive-shaped huts from saplings and leaves in just a few hours. The foragers hunt for duiker (an African antelope) and monkey meat, and collect

Right: An Efe man uses tools to make an arrow for hunting. Below: Ituri farmers heat scrap metal on a forge made of forest materials (wood, leaves, vines, mud) and shape the metal into traditional *apapaus*—curved knives they use for digging, cultivating, food preparation, and other purposes.

Foragers' camps are often on the edges of the farmers' fields. The two groups live close to each other for about seven months of the year.

honey and some other items from the forest for trade with the farmers. During planting and harvest seasons, the foragers also work in the farmers' fields. In return, the farmers trade food from their fields and manufactured items such as clothing, pots, and iron tools. Sometimes the two groups argue about the terms of their exchanges, but usually they live together peacefully, while keeping separate identities and lifestyles. Each group is important to the other and they often take part in each other's weddings, funerals, and celebrations.

The useful *apapau* (right) and a spear are two of a forager's typical tools.

Foragers and farmers celebrate together.

Andimau is an Ituri Forest farmer. His family and other families who speak the same language call themselves Lese. The forest shelters other groups of farmers too: the Bila, the Budu, the Mamvu, the Ndaka, the Beru, and the Bali. Each group has its own language and its own cultural traditions, but they live in similar ways. Andimau's small village, typical of Lese farmers, is made up of his extended family—his wife, his three sons, their wives, and their children.

Forest vines, lianas, are split and used to bind timbers and saplings to make the frames for houses.

They live in several small houses, each with two or three rooms. The farmers make the frames for their houses from timbers and saplings from the forest, and cover them with mud. Large leaves are used for roofs. All the materials for Andimau's house come from the forest surrounding the village.

Villagers weave mats, baskets, and other items from forest plant material.

On this morning Andimau, his wife Undekila, and one of their grandsons, eleven-year-old Gamiembi, have planned a trek to a camp in the forest about a four-hour walk from their village. There, Andimau and another Lese villager, Karoembi, have built a trap for fish—a weir—in a small river near the camp. If this fish trap has worked, their families will have plenty of fish to eat.

Gamiembi is excited that his grandparents are taking him along, and as the other villagers begin their everyday tasks—working in the garden, fetching water, preparing food, weaving baskets and sleeping mats—the three travelers prepare to leave. They sit in a small cluster to eat the leftovers from the previous evening's meal—boiled and mashed **plaintains**, fish, and manioc leaves cooked in palm

Efe foragers show the leaf packets they use for carrying honey, spices, or other items.

oil and seasoned with hot peppers and salt. Then Undekila fills a basket with a bunch of plantains, some large manioc tubers, a bottle of palm oil, three pots, cooking knives, a small *apapau*, an ax, and several neat leaf packets holding small amounts of salt, hot peppers, and soap. Andimau checks the arrows in his quiver, straightening their shafts and making sure the arrowheads are sharp and firmly attached. Gamiembi finds a smaller basket and packs it with more food and an empty jug to hold water when they reach the camp. They won't take along a water supply as there are plenty of streams and springs in the forest. When the baskets are ready, they hoist them onto their backs. A strap is stretched across their foreheads and its ends are attached to the basket, so the travelers'

Villagers often carry very heavy loads on their backs, with a strap—a tumpline—pulled across the head for support.

arms will be free as they walk. Undekila and Gamiembi start out, walking toward the village gardens and the forest beyond. Andimau follows, carrying his bow and quiver of arrows, and a machete—a large knife that he'll use to clear away brush blocking the trail.

The trail leads out of the village and through the village's last garden. It was planted the previous year and still provides some food from bushy manioc plants and large plantain trees loaded with unripe fruit. Next they pass through the village's new garden, where they will plant and harvest food during the next year or two. The larger trees have been cut and piles of brush have been partially burned as the villagers start to farm this area. Manioc sprouts and freshly planted plantain shoots poke up between the fallen trees. Manioc is an easy crop for the Lese farmers. They cut a 2- or 3-inch (5- or 7.5-cm) piece of manioc stalk, bury it in the ground, and wait for it to sprout. When the spring rains begin, they will plant peanuts and maize, using seeds stored from the last year's crop. In one of the village houses several ears of corn have been saved for planting. They hang down from the ceiling above the cooking fire, where the smoke protects them from insect damage.

Several crops may be planted in the same field; maize (corn), plantains, rice, and manioc are all growing in this mature garden.

Farmers cut up a manioc stalk and toss one or two pieces into a hole to sprout. The plant tops may wither in the dry season, or be scorched when the farmer burns the field, but the underground roots and tubers will grow again when the rains begin.

For many generations, Ituri farmers have practiced swidden agriculture: clearing and burning an area of forest, farming it for a few years, and moving on to a new area.

Toward the end of the dry season, the garden is a mass of cut vegetation waiting to be burned.

Any remaining vegetation is gathered by hand and piled up to be burned again. Large timbers are left in the fields, and the farmers plant around them.

The Lese practice **swidden agriculture**—a common farming method in tropical forest regions. Each year, they cut down an area of forest and leave the vegetation to dry in the hot sun during the three-month dry season, from December through February. Then they burn the brush and dried vegetation to clear the land. In March, when the rains begin, the men and women plant crops

The vegetation is burned, leaving behind ashes that will fertilize the farmer's crops.

Lese women chop up the timbers to use as firewood through the year.

between the larger logs that were not burned in the fire. Those logs will be used as firewood during the year. Lese usually don't plant in the same plot of land for more than two years. Soils in the Ituri, as in other tropical rain forests, are very poor in nutrients. Most of the nutrients are tied up in the living trees and other plants. When forest cover is cut down, the soil becomes depleted after

When the field is ready, a hoe is used to make holes for planting seed crops such as maize and peanuts.

A seed is dropped into each hole and covered with soil. Gardens are often planted two or three times, and so plantains, bananas, or some other crops may already be growing there.

only a few plantings and can't produce good harvests. The gardens are abandoned; they are left to lie **fallow,** or unplanted, for twenty years or more, and then they may be cleared again and replanted. In the first few years, quick-growing forest plants move into the abandoned garden. Later they give way to larger trees. Gradually, if undisturbed, the plot becomes mature rain forest once

The young crops have to be weeded, or else they may be crowded out by competing plants. Rice, manioc, and squash are growing in this garden. Efe and Lese together harvest rice crops or peanut crops. Plantains, manioc, and some other crops are harvested through the year. The large bushy plants between the rice plants are mature manioc plants.

again. The regrowth of the rain forest may take many decades, but as soon as a garden is abandoned, the process begins. However, if large tracts are cleared with huge, modern, forest-leveling equipment, they may not ever recover. The cleared area is too large and the rain-forest plants are unable to return before the thin soil erodes and becomes unsuitable for most native plant and animal species.

Vegetation moves in and grows quickly in areas that had once been cultivated.
Unless the plants along a trail are cut back, the trail is soon lost to the forest.

Andimau, Undekila, and Gamiembi pass through their new garden and
follow the trail out into an area of dense brush. This part of the trail is hot and
unpleasant, and the travelers are attacked by thorns and insects. Gradually, the
trail becomes more shaded with taller trees overhead, but the vegetation on the
forest floor is still thick. Gamiembi and his grandparents are walking back past

old, overgrown garden plots. Soon they reach the place where their village had been a few years earlier, on top of a hill. The land around the village was cleared and planted while they lived there. But when all the land within easy walking distance was exhausted, the people moved the village about a mile away, where they would have a new area to clear and plant.

As the travelers walk through the old garden plots, they can see the different stages of returning, or **secondary forest**. All through the Ituri there are patches of secondary forest that have been created by Andimau and other farmers. The size and type of plants growing in each of the patches reveal how long it has been left to regrow. This patchwork of mature and secondary forest has probably existed in the Ituri for as long as people have planted there. Today these areas of secondary growth are a good resource for both forest animals and humans. Some animals, such as the crowned guenon and the blue duiker, are adapted to these secondary

The six duiker species that live in the Ituri are often prey for foragers.

habitats and thrive here. This means that hunters in the Ituri can find more prey here than in mature forest areas. And, as Gamiembi and his grandparents make their way through the area, they hear the call of a beater leading a group of Efe hunters through the nearby brush. The Efe are the foragers who live alongside the Lese farmers in the northern and eastern parts of the Ituri Forest. Several groups of foragers—the Sua, the Aka, and the Mbuti, in addition to the Efe— live in the Ituri. Each group speaks its own dialect that is similar to the language of the farmers with whom they share a section of forest.

Efe foragers gather to plan where to hunt prey.

Dogs are important on Efe hunts. Often one is outfitted with a wooden clapper that makes noise as the dog moves through the forest. The noise scares out hiding animals, and also helps the hunters keep track of the dogs.

The Efe are on a *mota*—a group hunt in which from five to fifteen men and boys and a few dogs search the forest for sleeping or hiding animals. The noise and commotion made by the beater and the dogs flush out forest animals. The hunters, walking ahead of the beater with their bows and arrows ready, shoot the fleeing animals.

Efe men climb high into the canopy to search for honey—a food both the Efe and the Lese prize.

The Efe are among the smallest people in the world. The men average about 4 feet 8 inches (1.43 m) in height and the women about 4 feet 6 inches (1.37 m). Their small size enables them to move through tangled forest vegetation and climb forest trees more easily than their taller neighbors, the Lese.

As the hunters file quietly past the walkers on the trail, Andimau greets them. He calls out to one, Ite, to ask if he has been to the camp where Andimau built his weir. Andimau wants to know if the weir is trapping lots of fish. Ite answers that his group passed through the camp the day before, but that only a few small fish were being trapped each day and there weren't even enough fish to feed Karoembi's family, who are staying at the camp. If it hadn't been for the Efe hunters, and the animals they had killed that day, Karoembi's family would have had neither fish nor meat to eat with their manioc.

What a disappointment for Andimau! His hard work in building the weir has not paid off with rich rewards as he had hoped. As Ite rejoins the hunters, Andimau calls after him, telling him to come back to the camp and bring some honey for all of them to eat. But Andimau wonders if the weir is really trapping so few fish, or if perhaps some of the fish are being stolen.

The trail continues down a steep ravine, across a large stream and up the other side. At the bottom of the ravine the trail is very muddy and the party walks along logs other travelers have cut and placed on top of the mud. Many patches of swampy, muddy terrain dot the forest. Some, like this one, are small, while others, especially those along larger rivers, spread over an extensive area. Fish, freshwater crabs, and other animals make their home in this **riparian**

The forest is dotted with patches of swampy, muddy terrain.

SHOEBILL STORK
Balaeniceps rex

RANGE: Swamplands of eastern Africa, central Africa

HABITAT: Freshwater swamps, pools, deep channels in large swamps

SIZE: 47 in (120 cm) in height

WEIGHT: 11-13 lbs (5-6 kg)

FOOD: Fish, amphibians, reptiles; also small birds and mammals

LIFE SPAN: Unknown

REPRODUCTION: 1-3 white-shelled eggs

RAIN FOREST LEVEL: Forest floor, swamplands

Shoebill storks often live in wetlands or near slow-moving waterways. Their long, stiltlike legs allow them to wade through shallow water, and their long beaks are specially adapted for catching prey. There are eight stork species in tropical Africa, and of all these storks, the shoebill has the largest, broadest beak.

Shoebills are masters of patience. They stand silently, unmoving, until a large fish, snake, frog, or even turtle swims by. At precisely the right moment they plunge their beaks into the water and snatch their dinner.

The shoebills' multipurpose beak is used, too, as a bucket for transporting water. Shoebill parents scoop up water in their beaks and carry it to their nests where they shower their chicks who are too young to venture out, but in need of relief from the extreme heat.

habitat. Shoebill storks (*Balaeniceps rex*) are residents of large swamps. They wait, standing perfectly still, and then use their oversize beaks to ambush large fish, snakes, turtles, and other aquatic animals traveling along deep channels in the swamp. The shoebill's stand-and-wait hunting method is successful only in tropical waters where fish are abundant.

As they climb up out of the ravine, the travelers hear a crashing sound in the trees above. Gamiembi looks up and calls out "*Mbengi*!"—the Lese name for the crowned guenon (*Cercopithecus pogonias*). Crowned guenons are one of the enormous variety of primates that live in the Ituri. There are chimpanzees,

CROWNED GUENON
Cercopithecus pogonias

RANGE: South Cameroon to Congo Basin
HABITAT: Secondary forest
SIZE: Males 20-26 in (50-66 cm) in height;
females 15-18 in (38-46 cm)
WEIGHT: Males 6.6-13.2 lbs (3-6 kg);
females 4-6.6 lbs (1.8-3 kg)
FOOD: Fruits, insects
LIFE SPAN: 20-30 years
REPRODUCTION: Gestation approximately
5 months, usually one offspring
RAIN FOREST LEVEL: Canopy

The crowned guenon is a member of a large group of African long-tailed monkeys, and for a canopy-dwelling monkey, having a long tail is a matter of survival. The slender, graceful guenons use their long tails the way tightrope walkers use their outstretched arms—to keep their balance. Crowned guenons also have strong, grasping hands and feet that help them move quickly along branches and from tree to tree. They live and also find their food—mostly fruits and insects—high up in the forest canopy.

Guenons live in social groups made up of several adult females and their offspring, and usually one adult male. The members of a troop usually stay close together, but when food is scarce, they may spread out through the forest. If there is confusion about the boundaries of each group's territory, the loud, long-distance calls of the adult males usually settle the matter.

the olive baboon, three species of colobus monkey, six species of Cercopithecus monkey (including the crowned guenon), and two species of the large Cercocebus monkeys called mangabeys. The Ituri is home to more mammalian species than most other areas in Africa, and this is especially true of primates.

Each of the many different species of monkeys that live in the Ituri occupies a particular **niche** in the **ecosystem**, that is, each specializes in different resources. This reduces competition for food among the monkey species as each one forages for its own specific food at specific levels in the forest and at specific times of the day or night. The crowned guenon that Gamiembi spotted, along with redtail

ABYSSINIAN BLACK-AND-WHITE COLOBUS MONKEY
Colobus guereza

RANGE: Eastern and central African forests
HABITAT: Forest
SIZE: 18-28 in (45-70 cm) body; 20-36 in (52-90 cm) tail
WEIGHT: 12-32 lb (5.4 to 14.5 kg)
FOOD: Leaves, fruits, flowers
LIFE SPAN: 20 years in the wild, 29 in captivity
REPRODUCTION: Gestation: 6 months; one offspring born every 20 months
RAIN FOREST LEVEL: Emergent level and upper canopy

Black-and-white colobus monkeys live high in the forest's emergent level. They leap from limb to limb in the tallest trees, trailing long black-and-white hair from their backs as if wearing capes. Most of the day, however, they sit quietly, sunning, grooming, feeding, and digesting. Their specialized digestive system enables them to eat large quantities of foliage at the trees' emergent level. These leaves can be toxic to other monkeys.

Black-and-white colobus births occur mainly during rainy season. The newborns have all-white hair that gradually darkens so by the time they are 17 weeks old, they have adult coloration. Growing up in the trees means that babies need to be able to cling firmly with their hands and feet to their mother or another adult monkey, for babies are regularly handled by other females in the troop. This behavior is believed to strengthen social bonds among the females.

monkeys (*Cercopithecus ascanius*) and blue monkeys (*Cercopithecus mitis*), forage in areas of secondary growth, like that surrounding Andimau's abandoned village. The reason may be that these animals are all **frugivores**—fruit makes up a large part of their diet, and some trees that grow in areas of secondary growth produce fruit year round rather than in just one season. The Abyssinian black-and-white colobus (*Colobus guereza)* is a **folivore** and eats a greater proportion of leaves. Because plants in secondary forest grow quickly, producing a lot of new leaves and branches as they compete for the available sunlight, the black-and-white colobus is often found living here, too.

At the top of the ravine the trail levels off and follows a ridge. The forest is more open here, with much less vegetation at ground level. It is cooler, too,

because sunlight is trapped by the leaves of the giant hardwood trees in this part of the forest. The size of the trees shows that it has been a long time since anyone cleared a garden on this side of the ravine. Rofo (*Brachystegia laurentii*) and ato (*Cynometra alexandrii*) trees make up 40 percent of the canopy in this part of the Ituri. They can grow to heights of 150 feet (45.5 m) or more and their trunks are covered with creepers and lianas—growing vines that use tree trunks as ladders to reach the canopy. The rofo and ato trees have few leaves or branches except at their very tops, which spread like umbrellas to catch the sunlight that is available only there—far above the ground. To support their

To cut down a tall, buttressed tree, Efe and Lese men build a perch so they can cut higher up along the trunk, where the tree is not as thick.

grand height and top-heavy profiles, the trees grow very thick near the base, and form huge buttresses for stability. Their roots are very shallow, but they grow out in every direction to draw nutrients from the poor soil of the rain forest. The thin soil—just a few inches deep—is replenished only by decaying vegetation that lies everywhere on the forest floor. This decaying material—called detritus—gives the forest its pungent, earthy smell.

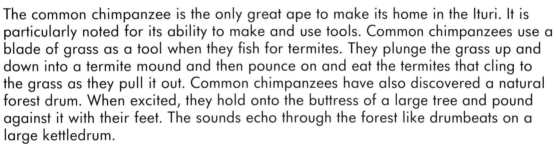

CHIMPANZEE
Pan troglodytes

RANGE: West-central Africa north of the Zaire River from Senegal to Tanzania
HABITAT: Tropical rain forests
SIZE: Males 30-36 in (77-92 cm); females 28-33 in (70-85 cm)
WEIGHT: Males 88 lbs (40 kg); females 66 lbs (30 kg)
FOOD: Fruits, foliage, and occasionally animal prey
LIFE SPAN: 40-45 years
REPRODUCTION: Gestation 230-240 days; 1 or, rarely, 2 offspring
RAIN FOREST LEVEL: Forest floor, understory, canopy

The common chimpanzee is the only great ape to make its home in the Ituri. It is particularly noted for its ability to make and use tools. Common chimpanzees use a blade of grass as a tool when they fish for termites. They plunge the grass up and down into a termite mound and then pounce on and eat the termites that cling to the grass as they pull it out. Common chimpanzees have also discovered a natural forest drum. When excited, they hold onto the buttress of a large tree and pound against it with their feet. The sounds echo through the forest like drumbeats on a large kettledrum.

Common chimpanzees live in communities of 15 to 120 individuals. During the day, they search for food—fruit and certain types of foliage and, occasionally, animal prey, including other primates and perhaps antelope. Each night, every member of the community makes a bed out of leaves and settles down to sleep high in the tree branches.

Loud primate screams now ring through the trees. From the commotion that follows, Andimau realizes that a group of chimpanzees must be hunting nearby. Common chimpanzees *(Pan troglodytes)* eat monkeys, pigs, antelope, and insects, although their diet consists mostly of fruit. Today these chimpanzees have chased a troop of monkeys up into the canopy. The monkeys are fleeing down their many escape routes through the continuous forest canopy. As the chase ends in failure, one adult chimpanzee uses the wide buttress of an ato tree as a drum, pounding its feet against the tree to create a thundering sound that echoes through the forest.

Goliath beetle

In this mature part of the forest, most of the action is far above the ground where Andimau, Undekila, and Gamiembi are walking. The sun's energy is trapped in the treetops so most plant growth takes place there; and the animals who feed on the plants are also high in the trees. While the forest floor is quiet, cool, and shady, the canopy more than 100 feet (30.3 m) above is hot from the sun's rays. Many plants have adapted to life in the canopy and use the big trees for support. Some canopy plants, called bromeliads, get all their nutrients directly from rainwater and never touch the ground at all. A number of arboreal mammals, reptiles, insects, and birds live almost their entire lives high up in the canopy, never coming down to the forest floor.

Insect life abounds in the canopy. Familiar insects, like mosquitoes that feed on the blood of animals and bees that feed on flower nectar, find food high up in the canopy, and so do many unusual and rare insects. Insects are the most diverse group of animals on earth. In the rain forest, there are more species of insects than of any other group of animals. And among the insect species, there are more types of beetles than any other insects. In the Ituri lives the heaviest beetle in the world, the Goliath beetle (*Goliathus cacicus*). Adults grow to be

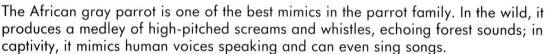

AFRICAN GRAY PARROT
Psittacus erithacus

RANGE: Central Africa
HABITAT: Lowland forest
SIZE: Height: 13.2 in (33 cm)
WEIGHT: 14-17.5 oz (400-500 g)
FOOD: Seeds, nuts, fruits, berries
LIFE SPAN: 60-80 years
REPRODUCTION: Average 3-egg clutch; breeding season variable
RAIN FOREST LEVEL: Canopy and emergent level

The African gray parrot is one of the best mimics in the parrot family. In the wild, it produces a medley of high-pitched screams and whistles, echoing forest sounds; in captivity, it mimics human voices speaking and can even sing songs.

The parrot is well adapted to forest life. When foraging, it often uses its feet and hooked beak to climb from branch to branch. Beak and feet serve as eating utensils, too. The feet, with two toes facing forward and two facing back, grasp the fruit. (Some parrots favor one foot, so perhaps, like humans, they are left or right "footed.") With its sensitive tongue, the bird positions a seed between its upper and lower beaks; the edge of the lower beak then pries open the seed. In this way, it cracks the forest's hardest seeds.

The parrots build nests inside hollow trees 100 feet (30 m) above the ground where the female lays and incubates the eggs until they hatch in three to four weeks. Both parents care for the young; the female keeping watch while the male supplies food. Even after the chicks fledge, at about ten weeks, the group may stay together as a family for up to a year.

6 inches (15 cm) long and weigh up to 0.75 of an ounce (2.2 g), which may not seem like much, but in the insect world, they are true heavyweights. Adults fly into the canopy to feed on fruit, but grubs live in the rotting vegetation of the forest floor. In the rain forest, insects are important **pollinators** and **decomposers** (recyclers), and also play important roles in the food chain as both predator and prey. The rain forest hosts so many different insect species that many have never been named or even seen by people.

Andimau cannot see the birds in the canopy, but he hears a burst of loud chattering sounds and he knows that a flock of African gray parrots (*Psittacus erithacus*) is flying overhead. Andimau also hears the splats and thumps produced by a troop of red colobus monkeys *(Colobus bodius)* dropping pieces of fruit from their treetop perches to the forest floor.

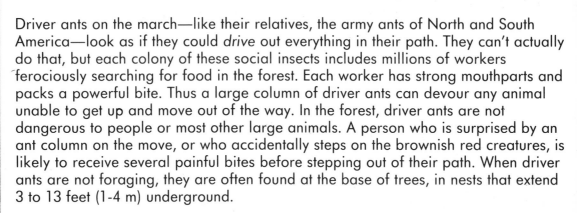

DRIVER ANTS
Genus: *Dorylus*

RANGE: Africa to tropical Asia
HABITAT: Rain forests
SIZE: Queens 1.5-2 in (39-50 mm); males and workers are smaller
WEIGHT: Colonies weigh under 44 lbs (20 kg); include over 20 million ants
FOOD: Animal prey, especially invertebrates
LIFE SPAN: Unknown
REPRODUCTION: A queen is capable of laying over one million eggs in a month.
RAIN FOREST LEVEL: Forest floor

Driver ants on the march—like their relatives, the army ants of North and South America—look as if they could *drive* out everything in their path. They can't actually do that, but each colony of these social insects includes millions of workers ferociously searching for food in the forest. Each worker has strong mouthparts and packs a powerful bite. Thus a large column of driver ants can devour any animal unable to get up and move out of the way. In the forest, driver ants are not dangerous to people or most other large animals. A person who is surprised by an ant column on the move, or who accidentally steps on the brownish red creatures, is likely to receive several painful bites before stepping out of their path. When driver ants are not foraging, they are often found at the base of trees, in nests that extend 3 to 13 feet (1-4 m) underground.

The forest floor seems a much quieter place than the canopy. But Undekila knows that isn't so. As they round a bend on the trail, Andimau spots a line of *siafu* in the trail. *Siafu* are driver ants that march through the forest in seemingly endless columns, preying on any small animals—including other insects—that are tiny enough or immobile enough for the ants to devour. Andimau and Gamiembi step around the *siafu*, but their footfalls alarm the ants, who spread out to defend their column. Undekila, traveling last in the line and carrying the heaviest load, can't avoid the ants, who now cover the trail. A few climb onto her feet and start up her legs. After running past their column to reach a safe area, she drops her basket and plucks the aggressive ants off her legs. Their large, sharp mandibles, or mouthparts, produce painful bites, but they can't do more than annoy humans and other large animals.

OKAPI
Okapia johnstoni

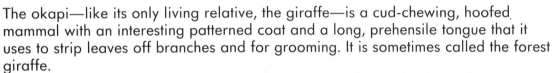

RANGE: Northeastern Zaire
HABITAT: Dense rain forest
SIZE: Shoulder height 5-6 ft (1.5-1.8 m)
WEIGHT: 465-550 lbs (210-299 kg)
FOOD: Tree leaves and young shoots, seeds, fruits
LIFE SPAN: 15 to 20 years in the wild, 25 in captivity
REPRODUCTION: Gestation 14-15 months; one calf every 2-3 years
RAIN FOREST LEVEL: Forest floor

The okapi—like its only living relative, the giraffe—is a cud-chewing, hoofed mammal with an interesting patterned coat and a long, prehensile tongue that it uses to strip leaves off branches and for grooming. It is sometimes called the forest giraffe.

The okapi is a shy, solitary animal that comes together with others of its species only to mate. Its dark color and the zebralike stripes on its rump camouflage its shape in the dappled light and shade of the dense rain-forest understory. This animal is so elusive, it was not discovered by scientists until 1900, making it one of the last large mammals to become known to the outside world.

The leaves of the many different plants growing in the mature forest provide the okapi's food. Most other hoofed animals feed on fruits or seeds, or the leaves of plants in forest clearings. The okapi, however, can digest the fibrous, often bad-tasting understory leaves; and this ability makes it a unique rain forest mammal.

Many larger animals also live on the floor of the mature forest. Most retreat into the forest shadows, hidden by leaves and their own camouflage, as the three travelers pass by. The okapi *(Okapia johnstoni)*, the national animal of Zaire, feeds on the leaves of shade-tolerant plants that live in the low light of mature forests. With its long **prehensile** tongue—like that of its **savanna** relative, the giraffe—the okapi strips leaves from small trees and saplings. Wild okapis live only in the Ituri. The Congo peafowl *(Afropavo congensis)*, the only true pheasant species in Africa, is another unusual animal that lives in the forest **understory**. The okapi, not discovered by scientists until 1901, and the Congo peafowl, not discovered until 1936, are the most famous animals of the Ituri.

The okapi's prehensile tongue

CONGO PEAFOWL
Afropavo congensis

RANGE: Northeastern Zaire, in the Congo Basin
HABITAT: Rain forest
SIZE: 26-28 in (64-70 cm)
WEIGHT: 3.8 lbs (1.7 kg)
FOOD: Seeds, fruits, insects
LIFE SPAN: Unknown
REPRODUCTION: Clutch size 3-6 eggs, 2-3 survive in each brood
RAIN FOREST LEVEL: Forest floor

The Congo peafowl is the only true pheasant in Africa. The bird was unknown until a visitor in 1913 noted an unusual feather in the headdress of an Ituri chief. A search for the source of the feather began, but it was not until 1936 that the bird was found in the Ituri Forest.

Today this rare bird, which lives only in the Ituri, is known as the Congo peafowl. Unlike other pheasants—such as the Indian peacock—the male lacks a long, resplendent tail to attract a mate in courtship displays. Instead, the black, blue, and green males attract mates—iridescent red-and-green females—using comparatively short, rounded tails.

During the day, Congo peafowl wander through the forest in search of food, often stopping under fruiting trees. They also eat ants and termites, and whirligig beetles that they pluck from the water. At night they fly up into the trees to roost safe from most predators.

YELLOW-BACKED DUIKER
Cephalophus silvicultor
RANGE: Gambia to Kenya, south to Angola and Zambia
HABITAT: Rain forest
SIZE: 45-56 in (65-85 cm) in height
WEIGHT: 100-176 lbs (45-80 kg)
FOOD: Fruit, leaves, shoots, buds, seeds
LIFE SPAN: 10-15 years in captivity
REPRODUCTION: Gestation 7½-8 months; 1 offspring
RAIN FOREST LEVEL: Forest floor

Duikers are small to medium-sized antelope. In Africa, there are seventeen duiker species; sixteen are forest dwellers, the last lives in bush areas or in savanna. The word *duiker* means "diver" in Afrikaans, and these animals do dive into the forest brush when threatened. Six species live in the Ituri: blue duiker, Peters' duiker, black-fronted duiker, bay duiker, white-bellied duiker, and yellow-backed duiker. The yellow-backed duiker is one of the largest and can be recognized by its yellow rump patch.

  Duikers are most abundant in areas of old secondary-growth forest. They are an important part of the forest food chain and make up a large portion of the bush meat caught by Efe hunters. Duikers are probably important prey for leopards, too.

Insectivores like the pangolin and aardvark feed on insects that live in the mat of decaying plant matter covering the forest floor. Duikers feed on fruits and other food items that fall from the trees or are dropped by animals feeding in the canopy above. Several duiker species live in both secondary and mature forest. The largest, the yellow-backed duiker (*Cephalophus silvicultor*), usually lives in mature forest. Another forest antelope, the spiral-horned bongo (*Tragelaphus eurycerus*), lives in clearings made by grazing elephants, or in areas of forest opened by Lese gardeners.

  As they make their way, Undekila stops and calls Gamiembi to look at a colorful mushroom growing beside the trail. Undekila remembers seeing an Efe

BONGO
Tragelaphus euryceros

RANGE: East, central, and west Africa
HABITAT: Rain forest
SIZE: 87-92 in (220-235 cm) head-body length
WEIGHT: Male 530-890 lbs (240-405 kg);
female 460-558 lbs (210-253 kg)
FOOD: Folivore
LIFE SPAN: 9 years in captivity
REPRODUCTION: Gestation 282-285 days; usually 1 offspring
RAIN FOREST LEVEL: Forest floor

The bongo is the largest forest antelope in the world. Both males and females have thick, spiral horns and a short, stiff mane running down their backs. These distinctly colored animals do not live in large herds like most of the antelope that roam the African plains, but instead live in smaller groups, usually of fewer than 20 animals. They are diurnal, browsing for food during the day.

Bongos are usually hard to find; they are swift and shy. However, their preferred food is the young plant foliage that sprouts in areas where forest elephants have eaten or trampled the mature plants, where trees have fallen, or where gardens have been abandoned and the secondary forest is beginning to recover. The bongos pick out high quality leaves from the poorer surrounding vegetation. Thus bongos can sometimes be seen in the Ituri—in the patchwork areas created by native farmers and in areas disturbed by forest elephants.

An immense variety of mushrooms and other fungi sprout from the decaying mat of vegetation on the forest floor. These, and many of the tropical forest's plant and animal species, may contain chemicals with medicinal or other value.

woman make a tea made from this mushroom and give it to a Lese villager who was afflicted with epilepsy. Undekila tells Gamiembi about two Efe women who are skilled in the use of forest medicines and tells him to pay attention when they harvest and use plants. Scientists in lands far from rain forests have learned to value the knowledge of the local people, and many of our medicines come from rain-forest plants. Some plants produce chemicals that prevent **herbivores** from eating their leaves; small doses of these chemicals make effective medicines for humans. Quinine is made from the bark of the cinchona tree of the Peruvian

GABOON VIPER
Bitis gabonica

RANGE: Eastern central Africa through eastern South Africa
HABITAT: Rain forests
SIZE: 3-4 ft (1-120 cm); occasionally up to 7 ft (210 cm)
WEIGHT: Up to 18 lbs (8 kg)
FOOD: Ground-dwelling birds, mammals; occasionally toads, frogs
LIFE SPAN: Unknown
REPRODUCTION: Gestation 3 months; 24-60 offspring
RAIN FOREST LEVEL: Forest floor

Venomous snakes of the viper family live throughout Africa. The Gaboon viper is the largest species of viper in Africa. Yet, when lying on the forest floor, these huge, thick-bodied snakes are almost invisible. Their beautiful brown, yellow, black, beige, and purple pattern disguises their outlines. They are perfectly camouflaged in the leaf litter, where they lie in wait to ambush any prey that comes within striking distance. Their long fangs can inject a deadly venom into small mammals— and people as well, if they should wander too close.

rain forest. It is widely used to treat malaria, the most deadly disease in human history. Not all plant treatments used by indigenous people have been shown to be useful, but tropical forests may hold other not-yet-discovered medical resources.

Andimau, walking ahead of Undekila and Gamiembi, spots a large viper in the trail. He waits for them to catch up and warily points it out. It is a Gaboon viper (*Bitis gabonica*), the largest viper in Africa. The colorful pattern of its scales makes it almost disappear in the leaf litter of the forest floor. If Andimau had not spied the viper, they could have stepped on or startled the snake and it might have struck to protect itself. Its venom is fatal to humans. Gamiembi picks up a stick and throws it at the snake, which quickly slithers off into the forest, allowing the three to continue down the trail.

The only way to cross some of the many rivers and streams in the forest is to use a fallen tree as a bridge. Sometimes trees are purposely cut so that they will fall and bridge the river.

In a weir, fish are trapped in a sieve or net made of saplings lashed together closely on a frame of logs.

Andimau, Undekila, and Gamiembi are close to their destination. They can hear water flowing through the weir. The sun is high in the sky and they are eager to make camp and cool off in the river. Undekila and Gamiembi cross the river on a tree trunk that has been cut down to serve as a bridge, while Andimau goes to check his weir. A weir traps fish by forcing the river's flow into a narrow channel where it must pass through a sieve, or net, made of saplings lashed together on a frame of logs. The water flows through the sieve,

The river water rushes through the weir, but the fish are trapped—if the weir works.

but the fish are trapped. Andimau and his partner, Karoembi, built their weir using logs and large leaves from the forest. However, the weir is not working. Andimau realizes no one has been stealing the fish; the fish are not being caught. Somehow most of the fish are getting through the sieve, or passing under it; or perhaps the fish are able to swim back upstream and escape the weir. Their clever idea isn't as effective as they had hoped. To make the weir work as it is supposed to, Andimau thinks they need to repair it carefully, making the holes smaller so the fish cannot escape. He will talk to Karoembi the next day and decide what to do.

Traditional ways of fishing, hunting, and farming do not produce large amounts of food quickly. The people work with simple tools, such as machetes, axes and hoes; few have guns or modern equipment. Yet small, sparsely spread populations—like the Lese and the Efe of the Ituri—have supported themselves for centuries in the rain forest. Their traditional methods do not threaten or endanger the survival of the forest species they hunt, fish, or gather. However, growing populations on the edges of the forest, a demand for bush meat (meat from wild animals) in towns and cities, and easier access to guns and other weapons have led to overhunting of animals in some areas. This is happening in parts of the Ituri, and in other tropical forests.

Other problems threaten the Ituri, too. Once many elephants roamed the forest near Andimau's weir. Now it is a full day's walk to reach the areas where the elephants can still be found. The demand for ivory tusks has led to large-scale poaching in recent years. While Efe and Lese once killed forest elephants (*Loxodonta africana*) for meat and for the respect they could earn as hunters, today nearly all the elephants killed in the Ituri are victims of poachers seeking only ivory. Now the Efe have to travel far from the roads that border and cut through the Ituri to find forest elephants—too far to make it worth the effort to hunt them for food. And, since trying to sneak up on an elephant and thrust a spear into its leg can be difficult and risky, the Efe now rarely practice their traditional elephant hunt.

The elephants probably have a greater impact on the **habitats** in the Ituri than any other animal species—except for human beings. As elephants lumber through the tangled vegetation of the secondary forest, they clear large, tunnel-like trails. With their enormous appetites, they consume over 200 pounds (90

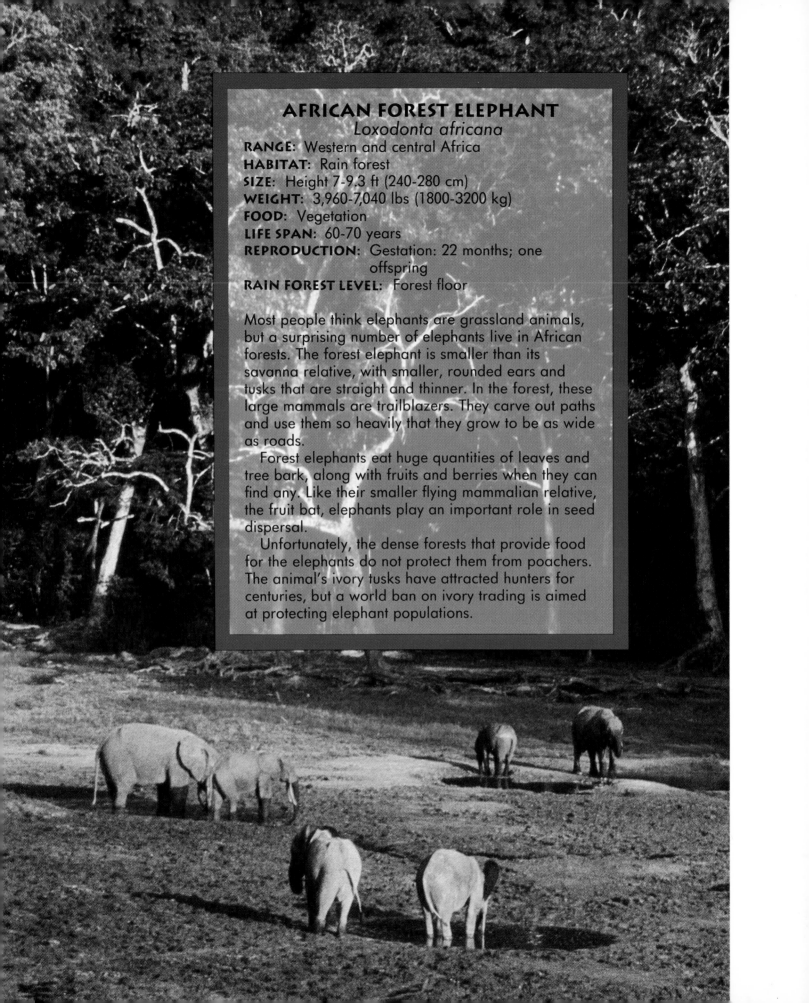

AFRICAN FOREST ELEPHANT
Loxodonta africana

RANGE: Western and central Africa
HABITAT: Rain forest
SIZE: Height 7-9.3 ft (240-280 cm)
WEIGHT: 3,960-7,040 lbs (1800-3200 kg)
FOOD: Vegetation
LIFE SPAN: 60-70 years
REPRODUCTION: Gestation: 22 months; one offspring
RAIN FOREST LEVEL: Forest floor

Most people think elephants are grassland animals, but a surprising number of elephants live in African forests. The forest elephant is smaller than its savanna relative, with smaller, rounded ears and tusks that are straight and thinner. In the forest, these large mammals are trailblazers. They carve out paths and use them so heavily that they grow to be as wide as roads.

Forest elephants eat huge quantities of leaves and tree bark, along with fruits and berries when they can find any. Like their smaller flying mammalian relative, the fruit bat, elephants play an important role in seed dispersal.

Unfortunately, the dense forests that provide food for the elephants do not protect them from poachers. The animal's ivory tusks have attracted hunters for centuries, but a world ban on ivory trading is aimed at protecting elephant populations.

Poachers seeking ivory kill the elephants for their tusks and often leave the huge bodies to rot in the forest.

kg) of vegetation each day, sometimes pulling down small trees with their trunks to reach the foliage at their tops. No one knows how the forest would be affected if this important member of its animal community disappeared. A worldwide ban on the sale of ivory is now in place, so perhaps elephant populations will increase and the animals will again be seen in the forest near the river.

As elephants pass through a muddy area, they leave behind enormous footprints that soon fill with water.

Undekila and Gamiembi greet Karoembi and his family at the camp, and Gamiembi shows them how he bravely chased away the viper they encountered on the trail. Andimau soon joins them, his unhappy face telling them the weir held just a few small fish. Karoembi shares his disappointment, and the two make plans to try to improve the trap.

Karoembi tells the new arrivals that a few Efe foragers had passed that morning, on their way to harvest *isou* (a forest yam) at an area near a large rock outcropping where they know the plant grows. The Efe planned to camp at a natural rock shelter there. Andimau, still thinking about his weir, complains to Karoembi, "They probably went to eat honey, while we sit here with grumbling stomachs because the fish are not falling into our trap." Karoembi laughs and replies, "They wouldn't cut a honey tree now. It's too early in the season, and the hive would have no honey. They went to find *isou*."

Rock outcroppings create microhabitats for particular forest plants and animals.

The Ituri is dotted with outcroppings of granite, some large enough to rise above the canopy and be visible from the air. And, as with all other Ituri **microhabitats**, some animal and plant species (such as the *isou* plant) specialize on the particular resources available at rock outcroppings. *Isou* is a popular food for the Efe. It is one of the few wild sources of carbohydrates in the forest and was probably an important part of the Efe's diet before cultivated foods like manioc, plantains, and corn were introduced.

One of the Ituri's most specialized mammals is the aardvark (*Orycteropus afer*). Known as nature's bulldozer, the nocturnal aardvark uses its large claws to dig up its only source of food, ants and termites. Aardvarks have no incisors or canine teeth, instead relying on their long sticky tongues to snag their food. Today aardvarks are the only living member of an entire order of mammals (Tubulidentata).

The aardvark

As evening approaches, Karoembi helps Andimau set up a wooden frame and cover it with leaves, to make a lean-to-style house. Everyone is hungry and eager to share a meal of boiled plantains with the weir's small catch of fish fried in palm oil. Later, as Andimau and the others fall asleep, the forest takes on its nighttime character. It is very dark. The moon has not yet risen, and there are no city lights to provide a glow on the horizon. In fact, as during the day, the horizon is not visible through the trees.

The forest comes alive with the activity of nocturnal animals. In the canopy above the Lese camp, a small primate called a potto (*Perodicticus potto*) crawls out from its sleeping chamber inside a hollow tree to forage for insects and other small prey. While hunting, these shy creatures must also be alert for their own enemies such as the leopard, a predator that roams the forest at night looking for food. Leopards,

POTTO
Perodicticus potto

RANGE: West African coast, western central Africa
HABITAT: Tropical rain forests
SIZE: 12.5 in (32 cm) head-body length, plus 2 in (5 cm) tail
WEIGHT: 30-60 oz (850-1600 g)
FOOD: Fruits, insects, birds, bats, rodents
LIFE SPAN: 15 years in captivity
REPRODUCTION: Gestation 170 days; 1 offspring
RAIN FOREST LEVEL: Canopy

Pottos—also called bush bears or tree bears—are nocturnal, tree-dwelling primates that sleep by day in tree hollows and emerge at night to find food. Unlike other primates that speed along tree branches and up and down tree trunks, pottos are slow, careful climbers. They move unnoticed through the canopy, clinging to the branches, sometimes proceeding along the undersides of tree limbs. Their slow speed doesn't affect their ability to forage for fruit and the many foul-tasting insects like caterpillars, butterflies, and beetles that make up their diet. These irritant insects are not the prey of choice for many animals; but pottos are adapted to use them as food.

Should a potto be pursued by a forest predator—a leopard, genet, or mongoose—its escape options are limited. But when threatened, the potto can drop to the forest floor to escape, or curl up and defend itself using the spikes on the nape of its neck.

along with genets and mongooses, are the Ituri's main **carnivores**. Andimau, restless after the excitement of the day, stirs from his sleep and listens to the nocturnal activity surrounding their small camp. The sounds create a symphony—of calling insects, fluttering fruit bats circling over the roof of the hut, and water flowing through the weir in the distance.

Fruit bats and other frugivores are nature's gardeners; they disperse seeds throughout the forest. Each animal swallows seeds as it feeds on fruit. Many seeds have a hard covering that protects them from being digested by the animal. The frugivores cough up the hard seeds or they are passed through the animals' system and deposited with their feces. In a single night, a colony of fruit bats can carry thousands of pounds of fruit around the Ituri Forest. Scientists have learned that seeds passed through the digestive system of a fruit bat are more likely to germinate than those that fall to the forest floor in ripe fruit.

AFRICAN LEOPARD
Panthera pardus

RANGE: Africa south of the Sahara; South Asia
HABITAT: Rain forests to arid savannas;
        mountains to suburbs
SIZE: 40-75 in long (100-190 cm)
WEIGHT: Males 82-192 lbs (37-90 kg);
        females 62-132 lbs (28-60 kg)
FOOD: Animal prey
LIFE SPAN: 12 years in the wild, up to
        20 in captivity
REPRODUCTION: Gestation 90-105 days;
        average litter 2-3 cubs
RAIN FOREST LEVEL: Forest floor and understory

Leopards are not the strongest cats, the fastest cats, or the best jumpers in the cat family, but they are very good at all these things. They are the decathletes of the cat family, adaptable to many different situations. They can survive almost anywhere— in semideserts, in rain forests, and even on mountain slopes—if they can find water, food, and cover. They are the largest predators, other than human beings, in the Ituri. Using strength, agility, and camouflage, leopards are successful hunters of small mammals and birds, and are also quite clever. In the Ituri, they occasionally prey upon larger mammals like yellow-backed duiker or okapi. Once they have captured their dinner they can carry smaller prey into the trees and hide it from other predators. Because they are generally solitary, and are nocturnal hunters, they are rarely seen by people.

Seeds dropped by fruit bats
are responsible for most of the
plants in recovering forest areas.

Large projects like building a fish weir are risky. They take time and effort, and sometimes fail.

Andimau and Karoembi wake early the next morning and set to work on their fish weir. If they can make it work, and are fortunate, they will then catch many fish. They will stay at the camp for a few weeks more, collecting fish and smoking it over fires to preserve it. Occasionally in that time, Undekila and Gamiembi will travel back to the home village, to take some of the fish to market and to get a new supply of manioc and plantains from their garden. When the rainy season starts, everyone will return home, leaving the river's rising waters to destroy the weir and wash its logs, branches, and leaves downstream.

If Andimau's plan is successful—if he and Karoembi fix the weir and catch many fish—they may return the following year and build another weir. If they

For centuries, the Ituri has been home to both foragers and farmers who—in sharing the forest's resources—have found a sense of kinship and a deep loyalty to each other and to the forest.

cannot get the weir to work, they may decide to leave weir-building to others who have done it before and know how to do it well.

On this day, life in the Ituri Forest will continue as it has for thousands of years. The Efe and Lese are comfortable in the forest. From their childhood they learn to identify its plants and animals, to feed themselves from its resources, and to make their homes on its soil. For all of us who live outside the forest, there is still much knowledge about it that remains to be revealed. We value the forest for what we may learn there, for the products that come from its

bounty, for its benefits for our health and its important role in our ecosystems, and for its beauty and majesty. For the Lese and the Efe, the forest is their home, the source of their livelihoods, the setting for their history, and the place in which their culture was born and continues to live and develop today. For all these values, each of us should do what we can to ensure that the Ituri and other tropical areas are protected—along with the rights of the Lese and the Efe, and all the other indigenous peoples who live in the rain forests of the world.

GLOSSARY

APAPAU— a small, traditional Lese tool consisting of a metal blade 10-15 inches (30-40 cm) long, sharpened on one edge, hooked at the end, and mounted on a short handle. It is used for digging, clearing vegetation, preparing food, and other tasks.

BIODIVERSITY—the range or variety of distinct living species, their genetic base and the ecosystems and ecological processes of which they are parts.

CANOPY—the highest level of the tall trees in a rain forest, where the tree branches spread out and produce many leaves to capture sunlight. Branches of neighboring trees become intertwined and form a continuous layer of vegetation that can stretch for many miles.

CARNIVORE—an animal that feeds primarily on meat or bones.

CRESPUSCULAR— active primarily at dawn and dusk.

DECOMPOSER—an organism that feeds by breaking down organic matter.

DIURNAL—active primarily during the day.

ECOSYSTEM— all the interacting parts of the physical environment and the biological community.

FALLOW—describes land that is allowed to lie uncultivated during the growing season after having been farmed in a previous year.

FOLIVORE—an animal whose diet is, in large part, leaves.

FORAGERS— people whose diet consists chiefly of foods collected from the surrounding environment. Foragers do not plant crops or keep domesticated animals like cows or sheep. They hunt, fish, and gather fruits, nuts, honey, leaves, roots, mushrooms, insects, eggs, and other items. Early people were foragers, before some began to plant crops and tend herds.

FRUGIVORE—an animal whose diet is, in large part, fruit.

HABITAT— the area in which an animal or plant normally lives, including the available resources (food, water, shelter, space) and potential threats, such as predators.

HERBIVORE—an animal, especially a large grazing animal, whose diet is, in large part, plants.

INDIGENOUS PEOPLES—people whose ancestors are recognized as having been the earliest human inhabitants of the area in which they still live.

INSECTIVORE—an animal whose diet is, in large part, insects.

MANIOC—a crop grown for food in the tropics. Both leaves and tubers (starchy, large, fleshy parts of the underground stems) are eaten. In the Americas, manioc tubers are often called *yuca*.

MICROHABITAT—a small, specialized habitat; specifically the parts of the habitat important to the daily activities of an individual, or that the individual encounters on a regular basis.

NICHE—the role of a species within its ecosystem; specifically, the total of its use of the living and nonliving resources in its environment.

NOCTURNAL—active primarily at night.

PLANTAIN—a large starchy fruit that resembles a banana. It is an important food in the tropics where it is a staple in the diet; as potatoes, bread, and rice are staples in other regions.

POLLINATOR—an animal species that transfers pollen from the anther to the pistil of a flower, thus fertilizing a seed plant.

POPULATION DENSITY—a ratio of the number of individuals in a population to the size of the area they inhabit. It reveals the degree of crowding. Low population density means a small number of individuals live in a large area. High population density means a large number of individuals live in a relatively smaller area.

PREHENSILE—having the ability to seize or grasp, especially by wrapping around something.

RIPARIAN—relating to the area along the banks and edges of a river, lake, or stream.

SAVANNA—a grassland with a few scattered trees and drought-resistant undergrowth, most often found in the tropics or subtropics.

SECONDARY GROWTH; SECONDARY FOREST—parts of the forest where the mature or climax forest has been disturbed or cut down, and the succession of plant communities has not yet returned to climax forest.

SWIDDEN AGRICULTURE—a farming method practiced widely in the tropics. Farmers clear a patch of forest in the dry season, allow the cut vegetation to dry, and then burn it and plant crops at the beginning of the rainy season. A field may be used for only one to three years before being left to lie fallow, often for ten to twenty years, or more.

TROPICAL RAIN FORESTS— warm, humid forests that lie within the tropical regions (Tropics of Cancer and Capricorn) near the equator, in areas of year-round warm temperatures and abundant rain.

UNDERSTORY—the part of the forest below the canopy. The understory is cooler and more shaded than the canopy because it receives little direct sunlight; the vegetation is often less dense because of the lack of sunlight. Plants in the understory often have very dark leaves that are adapted to make the most of the available dappled sunlight.

FOR FURTHER READING

BOOKS FOR YOUNG READERS

Baker, Jeannie. *Where the Forest Meets the Sea.* New York: Greenwillow Books, 1987.

Cherry, Lynne. *The Great Kapok Tree: A Tale of the Amazon Rain Forest.* New York: Harcourt Brace Jovanovich, 1990.

Forsyth, Adrian. *Journey Through a Tropical Jungle.* New York: Simon and Schuster, 1988.

Mallory, Kenneth. *Waterhole: Life in a Rescued Tropical Forest.* New York: Franklin Watts, 1992.

Mazer, Anne. *The Salamander Room.* New York: Knopf, 1991.

Weir, Bob, and Wendy Weir. *Panther Dream: A Story of the African Rainforest.* New York: Hyperion Books for Children, 1991.

PERIODICALS

Audubon magazine

International Wildlife magazine

National Geographic magazine

National Wildlife magazine

Ranger Rick magazine

Wildlife Conservation magazine

GENERAL REFERENCE BOOKS

Collins, Mark. *The Last Rain Forests—A World Conservation Atlas.* New York: Oxford University Press, 1990.

Denslow, Julie S., and Christine Padoch, eds. *People of the Tropical Rainforest.* In association with Smithsonian Institution Traveling Exhibition Service. Berkeley: University of California Press, 1988.

Head, Suzanne, and Robert Heinzman. *Lessons of the Rainforest: Selected Essays.* San Francisco: Sierra Club Books, 1990.

Kingdon, Jonathan. *Island Africa: The Evolution of Africa's Rare Animals and Plants.* Princeton: Princeton University Press, 1989.

Newman, Arnold. *Tropical Rainforests.* New York: Facts On File, 1990.

Wilson, E. O. *The Diversity of Life.* Cambridge: Harvard University Press: 1992.

MAGAZINE AND JOURNAL ARTICLES

Bailey, Robert C. "The Efe: Archers of the African Rain Forest." *National Geographic,* November 1989, pp. 664-686.

Hart, Terese, and John Hart. "Between Sun and Shadow." *Natural History,* November 1992.

Hart, T. B., J. A. Hart, and S. C. Thomas. "The Ituri Forest of Zaire: Primate Diversity and Prospects for Conservation." *Primate Conservation,* 7:42-44.

Wilkie, David, and Gilda Morelli. "Coming of Age in the Ituri." *Natural History,* October 1991.

Wilkie, D. S., and J. T. Finn. "Slash-burn Cultivation and Mammal Abundance in the Ituri Forest, Zaire." *Biotropica,* 22(1):90-99.

FOR MORE INFORMATION

Contact these organizations to learn more about the rain forests, and how you can work to preserve threatened habitats.

The Ituri Fund
Cultural Survival
c/o Ted MacDonald
215 First St.
Cambridge, MA 02142

Cincinnati Zoo Conservation Fund
c/o Penny Geary, Education Dept.
P. O. Box 19803
Cincinnati, OH 45220-8073

Conservation International
1015 18th St. NW–Suite 1000
Washington, DC 20036

World Wildlife Fund
1250 24th St. NW
Washington, DC 20037

National Wildlife Federation
1400 16th St. NW
Washington, DC 20036-2266

The Nature Conservancy
1815 North Lynn St.
Arlington, VA 22209

The Ituri Fund was established by a group of concerned anthropologists, ecologists, psychologists, and physicians to promote the health, education, and self-determination of the Efe and Lese peoples living in the Ituri rain forest in central Zaire. The goals of the Fund are to help the people provide education for their children and to establish a community health center. Literacy and health are essential for development planning that will affect this community's resources, traditional practices, and autonomy. They must speak for the forest, which they depend on for food, medicine, clothing, and shelter.

The Cincinnati Zoo Conservation Fund is committed to working closely with the Ituri Fund in helping the Efe and Lese peoples provide sound education, school supplies, and teacher salaries, in addition to supporting the community health center and pharmacy.

An area of disturbed tropical rain forest, like this now-abandoned Lese garden (foreground), can recover if enough biodiversity exists in the surrounding mature forest (background). The Lese way of living in the forest is a good model for us all: Natural resources used wisely and with care can provide a sustainable future for all life on earth.

INDEX

Page numbers in *italics* refer to illustrations.

ABOUT THE AUTHORS

DAVID JENIKE holds a B.S. in zoology and an M.S. in environmental science from Miami University in Ohio. He is a zoologist and environmental educator and assistant director of education at the Cincinnati Zoo.

MARK JENIKE graduated from Harvard University and earned a Ph.D. in anthropology from the University of California at Los Angeles. While working toward his doctorate, he lived among and studied the lifeways of the indigenous Efe and Lese peoples of the Ituri Forest. He is now a postdoctoral fellow at the University of California at Berkeley.